A Love Letter To My Emotions

Apoisi Chuilo Veronica

ISBN 978-93-5610-333-7
© Apoisi Chuilo Veronica 2022
Published in India 2022 by Pencil

A brand of

One Point Six Technologies Pvt. Ltd.
123, Building J2, Shram Seva Premises,
Wadala Truck Terminal, Wadala (E)
Mumbai 400037, Maharashtra, INDIA
E connect@thepencilapp.com
W www.thepencilapp.com

Author biography

Apoisi Chuilo, who also goes by the name Veronica is a twenty four year old student from Dimapur, Nagaland. She is currently pursuing her masters in English, and has a deep love for writing to express her inbuilt emotions she doesn't speak out loud. She says writing is her escape and finds comfort in it.

A Love Letter To My Emotions is her debut poetry book.

CONTENTS

The Mommy that I Know

My Mommy is the best,

Among all of the rest.

She loves and cares for me the most,

Never letting me know about the worst.

She smiles with the brightest eyes,

Making me laugh with blight dyes.

She calls me mad,

Whenever I'm sad.

She never wants me to cry,

But let me learn how to try.

I look unto the pictures and smile,

How she teaches me to be versatile.

Whenever I feel like I'm alone,

She reminds me where I belong.

Whenever I am lazy,

She drives me crazy.

She never shows us her tears,

For she never wants us to bear.

She says that she's always there to wipe my tears,

And I know I am blessed to have a Mommy like her.

She is all that I want to be with;

"Heaven! Don't you call her back."

My Bestie

Oh Bestie!

Where are you?

I've been longing to see you.

I miss every move of ours,

Of when we were together.

Oh Dear!

Sheer coincidence to meet you,

Don't know how we met.

Don't know how we started,

Don't know how we became so close.

And as we grow each day

The world will part our ways,

Yet we will still hold this bond.

Fun is always being with you

Your absence is me covered in garments,

I never thought that I would be caught.

Being a friend of yours I feel blessed,

For it is in you that I will find rest.

My life was adventurous,

When we were notorious.

I miss you like I've always been longing for water.

I yearn each moment together for its unforgettable,

Without you my world becomes lifeless,

As it paints itself as everything colorless.

Lovers Thought

Love is like beautiful scented flowers,

Which is filled with adorable colors.

Life seems beautiful,

When love is wonderful.

Choose your companions with care,

For you become who they are.

Love is filled with full of charm,

When it is surrounded by warm arms.

Don't let the crowd pressure you.

Stand for something,

Or you'll fall for anything.

Love is a tool,

For the fool.

Who can always write love poems or love letters,

Until it hardly matters.

I never knew what really love means,

Until I realized and understood my sins.

Love is when you take care of others,

Remember, it's nice even in the dark,

Be it in the streets or in the park.

Love doesn't always mean couples,

Love is anything but getting you in trouble.

Love your books; for it gives you wisdom.

Love your parents; for they live for you.

Love your friends, for they will be there.

Love your lovers; for they adore you.

Love your enemies; for they teach you.

But-

Never fall for pretenders,

Who'll steal your genders.

Be one of a kind,

Love won't mind.

Be the lover of all,

Carry it till you are old.

This is Me

A girl made of love.

I am a ritzy type of girl.

I know I'm not worth it,

Yet I don't play pretend games.

I am who I am meant to be,

And that is more than enough,

A little different, something you'll keep.

Just Being Real

Trust me, I am not rude.

I just say what you cannot.

When I fell at my worst,

I acted out to be at my best.

Then I made up my mind,

Maybe change is what I need.

That part is grown, this is me.

To be real, I need to live it.

Still Living

I am full of heartaches and poetry,

I still choose to live it then to run.

I know that joy comes from within,

It is not in my status or anything.

Even during the hard times,

Giving up will never be an option.

I will live more days than that.

Choosing

I live my life with my own rules.

Nobody can come to take it away,

May the toxicity of the world know that,

They can choose to love or despise me

There are things out of my control,

But I will choose what I can hold.

Feelings Caught

Now I smile with tears.

And I cry with my smile.

Things do change with time.

Somedays are harder than the rest,

But what growth is in worrying too much?

I know my heart will reside in yours,

And I will choose that over and over.

Ye

I choose to be a girl who picks adventure,

The world may make this part of me odd.

I don't care if you call yourselves weird.

Somedays I call myself stupid too.

All that matters is that you are wonderful,

And being odd was never wrong to begin with.

You never know

You'll not know what memories are fading inside of you until you look,

Maybe when you do, it's attractive because in those moments,

You'll see who you were unapologetically.

Stop insisting on clearing your head.

You need to untangle your heart that's been jumbled up.

It's all about one,

Belongs to ome,

And owns just one.

Just Go On

People say you realize what you lost after it's gone.

Well I know what I had,

And I'm glad it's gone.

It takes the deepest fall to know how far I'll rise.

Hate a little less for what you were not,

And love a little more for what you are.

In me

I will not let go of this pretty soul that you created in me.

For that love has always saved me, and always will.

After all- We've been through,

"FIRE" and "SMOKE".

So I'm gonna hold onto this hope even if the world gives up.

Though I'm thoroughly a mess,

Nothing compares until you live in me.

Broken yet secure

Once I felt as if someone had just ripped my heart out and broken it into pieces.

I burst into tears as you took me in your arms.

Because I was scared and utterly terrified.

Today it's like I found peace within you,

I am **broken yet secure**.

You did it all

Whenever you are angry over me,

I fell down, for I thought you did not care.

Left me astray to be on my own.

Time heals; so did I realize you always loved me first.

You always stood next to me.

Watching me and protecting me in every way.

Thank you so much for the love and care towards me.

My King

He loves me,

He cares for me,

He reminisces with me with His love towards me.

He respects me not just me but all.

He is the only one who gives enough chances.

He is a being with kindness.

He is my king.

My love.

My everything.

D

I know I'm a "Bootless Lass",

But at least I'm not some 'Insensate'.

So don't judge me until you know the real me.

"MY SCOWLNESS MIGHT KILL YOU".

Dreams Dreamt

Dreams that were once an imagination,

I discovered them to be real.

An amazement that filled my world in dreams is now a wonder that shines my day.

Moments that I've always dreamt now of a scene of reality.

'Dreams Dreamt' and now true, cause it's you.

Someone special

I smile for you,

I laugh because you make me,

I fantasize that you can make me feel it's true.

I wonder because you are in it.

I daydream in your thoughts,

Because you are the reason I live for.

Reverse

I have nothing much to say,

Remember I don't need anything.

Just your respect for mine.

I owe you, only when you owe me.

Who I am

I will never live to be someone I am not.

I will carry this beautifully.

I refuse to get lost in someone's dream.

Made with purpose, defined by grace,

I'm gonna live life fearlessly.

I will become who I am meant to be

Deep Rivers

I am everything you cannot see,

A sea of emotions lives inside my body.

You may call me a psycho,

Because you do not see what I see,

None can understand but I,

After all I have been the only one,

Swimming in my own ocean.

The world is dancing

Life's awesome they say,

When in times of enjoyment.

While they proclaim that life's hard to live .

When in times of suffering.

So I speak,

Why would you think you can judge?

Sit down and drink from you own cup.

And satisfy your worth of living.

Be the sun

When I open my eyes in the morning,

I want to thank the sun for the warmness.

As I bask, I don't want to complain.

All the glory that this Earth gives,

We want it but we often complain,

If you are the sun, you will know,

You shine so that there is light,

You don't want it, you need it.

I walk on a dusty road

Being frolic is what everyone says I am

And it's true

But it ain't my passion no more.

Just a mere-shot.

Sublunary

Sometimes it's better to change than to be the same jerk.
Still I chose to love you in silence,

For I feel no rejection.

When you happened

I'm wearing the smile you showed me how to wear.

Dressed in a fine design of what I sew,

For you taught me how to stitch.

A love letter to my emotions

All the parts of me has been made by me

Under nights of countless storms,

I was built under harsh weather.

They say I am rough on the edges

But I can't choose to heal overnight.

I am tender yet so fierce.

If they choose not to see me,

I cannot bind them to me.

I run to you

Draped by the love that you gave,
There is nothing more I want.
All I could ever dream of is to be with you back and now.

Chamber walls

There was a girl who tried everything just to find herself back, Looking around for the lost soul,

Talking to herself about everything that's happening.

Smiling on her own like an idiot.

Then find herself crying at some corner, all alone .

For even after everything she was still inside chamber walls

.

Last hour

Gone are the days when we were young,

Gone are the days when we laughed every little moment.

Gone are the days when we found ourselves everywhere.

If I had known, would I stay?

I know I need to move from there,

But even if it's for a fragment,

Take me back to the lost hour.

Will you come for me

I walk pass those paths and it reminds me of you.

I looked for your footsteps but it was long gone.

Everytime I think of you, it feels like as though you are running After me, calling out my name.

I've been looking for your eyes to look into mine.

When will you find that I've been starving for you.

I spiral across life

The touch of the waves,

The sight of trees.

The sound of laughter,

The feeling of being fully alive makes me wander even more than I ever did,

And that really made me feel what love and living meant.

I reach for you

Why do I still clasp over and over to our memories,

When all I find is a missing me; lost all on my own.

C

There is something magical about that one being,

For whenever my thoughts turn to it,

It puts the whole world on **"Cherry mode"**.

Days gone

Days gone.
The night fall,
And the soul rise.
The stars shines
While tears fall from the eyes .
Clouds moving round,
Heads going down,
Days went by.
While night stand by.
She bids goodbye,
And he let it go saying not to stand by.